# Fantasy
## Writing Prompts

This book belongs to:

_____
_____
_____
_____

© Creative Zebra Press

## Fantasy Writing Prompts for Creative Writers

Copyright © 2022 Creative Zebra Press

Creative Zebra Press
127 W Fairbanks Ave
Suite 363
Winter Park, FL 32789

Reproduction of these materials is prohibited without the written consent of Creative Zebra Press.

ISBN: 9798351171555

www.creativezebrapress.com

# How to Use This Book

Hey there!

We hope you enjoy using these writing prompts that were created to help you write amazing stories!

Use the space provided after each prompt to jot down notes and ideas for your story, then use a notebook to write it down. There are 20 pages included at the end of the workbook that you can use to write additional notes or to begin a story if you're somewhere without your notebook.

While using the prompts, please feel free to change names, genders, places, or anything else. These prompts are intended to inspire you, not to limit you.

This book was designed to get you started. You are the writer, these are your stories, so remember that you are completely in control. After all, the more you write the better you'll get.

Enjoy the writing process. Be creative. Share your stories with others.

Have fun writing!

*The Creative Zebra Team*

P.S. You'll find some vocabulary words at the end of the workbook to use in your writing. Also, on the very last page there's a list of common grammatical mistakes. Enjoy!

© Creative Zebra Press

# Elements of a Story

There are many elements to a story, but here are five to get you started: character, setting, plot, climax and resolution

**Characters** - the main character of your story is called the protagonist. Try to describe each character's life, emotions and physical appearance in a way that allows the reader to feel that they are real. If your reader loves or loathes your characters, then you've done a great job at describing who they are.

**Setting** - describe your setting's time and place. The setting could be a rustic kitchen in Italy in 1920. What would some of the contents of an Italian kitchen in the 1920s have? Your setting might also be another world where things are entirely different from ours. Imagine who lives there, what they do, how they live. Don't forget about factors such as the time of year and the weather. Help your reader feel like they are actually there.

**Plot** - this is the journey your characters take. What's happening in their lives, the conflicts they must deal with and their relationships with other characters. You should describe why they make the decisions they make. Are their decisions based on past life events (their **backstory**), fears about the future or something else?

Although you already know the plot of your story, reveal it to your readers slowly so that it's more interesting and engaging. To help develop your plot think about the message or feeling you would like to leave your readers with.

Your story should have a beginning, a middle, and an end. Before the end of your story you'll write the **climax** of your story, which is what your story has been leading up to, it's the most dramatic point in the story. This could be a confrontation, a discovery, bad news, or anything else that could be shocking, emotional, or unexpected. After the climax you'll write the aftermath or **resolution**, finally closing your story.

# Other Things to Consider

**Theme** - what's the theme of your story? Trust, betrayal, guilt, redemption, loss, empowerment, justice, love, friendship or something else? Consider mood here too. How do you want your reader to feel during different parts of your story?

**Point of view** - is your story written in first or third person? First person is written from the main character's point of view. Third person is omniscient. In other words, the writer is all knowing. The writer presents the views of all characters, as well as their thoughts and actions.

**Internal conflict** - does your character have something they are dealing with internally? It could be with another character, nature, their country, morals, or something else that is not in their control. How do they feel or struggle with this? How does their internal conflict affect the story?

**Dialogue** - use dialogue sparingly as it can be difficult for readers to follow. However, it is important to show how characters connect with each other, so it is necessary.

A Few Tips to Help You Become a Better Writer

Write what you know about, or spend time doing a little research.

The first few sentences of your story should be very compelling and **hook** your readers so that they'll keep reading in order to find out what happens. Be careful not to give the ending away though. Remember to reveal important story details to your reader, little by little, throughout the book.

Don't be afraid to have bad things happen to your main character. It can make for a much more interesting story. Be sure to incorporate lots of twists and turns in your story along the way.

Keep a notebook of ideas full of things that have happened or that you've heard. Eavesdrop on other people's conversations. Write about your dreams. Use these notes in future stories. You never know what might make a great story, so be sure to take inspiration from everywhere!

Read, read, read. Great writers read a lot!

The tree seemed to be whispering, "come closer, come closer," so they slowly and cautiously moved toward the tree, their curiosity getting the best of them. Then, they saw them, seven beautiful gems of various colors and sizes, sparkling in the darkness.

You're a trickster during medieval times. Your most recent scheme has you going from town to town slaying monsters. You become a hero. No one knows that you were the one that created the monsters in the first place.

All Princess Calliope ever wanted was a pet dragon. On her twelfth birthday her parents surprised her with a baby dragon. Now, as a young adult, the princess is discovering everything her dragon is capable of.

A child refuses to give his tooth to the tooth fairy. The tooth fairy has to resort to drastic measures.

You're a summoner. Everyone laughed at you when you could only summon very small things. Now, you're the one laughing as the whole city is swarmed by hundreds of thousands of bees.

You're at your first poetry reading. Halfway through, you notice a lot of commotion in the crowd. Turns out the poem you're reading is actually a magic spell.

Funglebunglemungle is actually the worst magician in the world. Every time he raises his wand, something goes wrong.

"Your own actions brought you here. I'm offering you a second chance, a do-over."

Your little brother runs into the house excited to tell everyone what he found in the woods.

With no hope of getting out the way they came in after the earthquake, the spelunkers go deeper into the cave and come across a map carved in the rock.

You're close to graduating with straight A's. You're led to the basement of the school where you see all the other top students looking just as confused as you are.

On your fifteenth birthday, your grandfather sits you down and explains to you that you are from a long line of wizards. He then presents you with a dusty old wizard's hat and robe. Your lessons start in the morning.

You are secretly a mermaid. Your friend, clueless about your hidden identity, signed you up for swim club at school.

**After begging them for years, your parents finally buy you a horse. The first time you get on your new horse to ride, it sprouts wings and takes off into the sky.**

As a witch that can turn animals into other types of animals, you decide to try this out on a human friend. Unfortunately, your spell backfires, and you become the animal you hate the most.

The knight finally rescues the princess from the dragon. After a few days with her, he tries to find the dragon so he can give her back.

You are the best detective in the world. Your secret is that you can speak to plants and animals.

You are a young villager. Your mother marries the king of the country. What is your new life like?

The whole city is gathered in front of the castle as the first woman is knighted by the king.

Jamie, a five year old boy, loved dogs. One evening, he mistakenly followed a pack of wolves into the forest.

While walking her dog, the old woman came across an injured bat on the sidewalk. She decided to rescue the poor thing. Unfortunately, the bat got startled and bit her right on the arm.

The pirate was amazed to see a cutlass, among many other things, being wielded by an octopus.

You finally find a dragon's lair after searching for one for months. You see lots of things you'd like to take home with you. Hopefully, the dragon doesn't show up while you're looking around.

During a trip to Iceland, you notice that the Northern Lights seem to be spelling out a message.

You're interning for a wolf trainer. His wolves have been used in several movies and television shows. It's exciting and fun until you notice that the wolves never blink or breathe.

People often forget that dragons didn't just exist in medieval times. What were they doing during the Industrial Revolution?

A powerful wizard gives you the chance to go back in time to change the outcome of one historical event. How do you use this opportunity?

A vampire, a werewolf, and a zombie walk into a mall.

The people in the land of Kisador are fed up with their oppressive ruler. They suspect he's a vampire so they team up to get rid of him forever.

When you become an adult you find out that you have superpowers based on your zodiac sign. How are you different now?

You borrow a pair of glasses from your grandfather's desk. You put them on and realize you can see through things.

A pyramid suddenly appears out of nowhere. As a famous archeologist, you're invited to be the first to investigate.

You're the best knight in the realm, but you have no idea what you're doing. Thank goodness for your whispering sword that tells you what to do in every situation.

You found a beautiful antique skeleton key in the old bed and breakfast where your family is staying. You and your little sister go around the house trying to figure out what it opens.

As Olivia approached her boyfriend's front door she heard howling coming from inside the home. She decided to peak in through one of the windows. The full moon illuminated the entire room. She gasped.

The storm blows your hot air balloon off course. After being violently thrashed about for what seems like an eternity, you find yourself in a beautiful kingdom among the clouds.

For the last ten years, you've been traveling the world in search of a missing box that contains something very special. You find it in the middle of the Sahara Desert. When you open the box, you're shocked at what you find.

Your parents buy a magic wand from a theme park. It's only supposed to work at the park, but when you get home, you find out it works even better than it did while you were there.

You've just opened your drive-through magic potion store. What are your top five sellers and what do they do?

A man has been sentenced to live the rest of his life in the dungeon of a castle. One morning, a wisp of smoke slips under the door. He hears a whisper, "if you promise to do what I ask, I'll set you free."

On the way to your first babysitting job, you come across a black leather bag. Inside you find all sorts of magical things to entertain the children with.

You've spent your entire life training to be an astronaut. Before your first mission, you're asked to sign a contract stating that you'll never talk about what you see up there. During the mission, you find out why they had you sign that contract.

You've been selected to travel back to medieval times. You're allowed to bring a backpack full of modern conveniences with you. What do you bring and how will you use them?

A mischievous twelve year old is given the opportunity to send a message to everyone on earth telepathically. It can be understood by everyone, regardless of the language they speak. What does the twelve year old say to cause the most chaos?

It's literally raining cats and dogs in your village, what do you do?

You've inherited a beautiful castle in Ireland. How did you get it and what will you do with it?

A genie grants you four wishes, you get to keep one, but must use the other three wishes for three other people. How do you use your wishes?

Walking along the beach near your house, you find a beautiful shiny rock. You take it home and put it on your shelf. Months later, it hatches.

Your parents invented the first camera. One day, while gazing at one of their first photos, you discover that you can travel back to the time and place that the photo was taken, and experience everything that happened at that time. How do you use this gift in the future?

You meet your favorite celebrity or fictitious character, you instantly become friends. What happens next?

The king's knights come into your village and demand that you be brought to them. What do they want?

At the magic carnival, your ping pong ball goes into a fishbowl and you win a tricky fish. Tricky fish are able to prank anyone you tell them to. You get to choose between a good fish or an evil fish, which do you choose and what will you ask it to do?

You and your friends discover a magical forest full of cupcake trees, candy trees, trees with cookies, bubblegum, and so much more.

Your family has always told you not to talk to the creepy merchant on the far side of town. However, you are desperate and know that he is the only one that can help you. You took the risk and now you regret it.

You think you're dreaming, but you're actually in your favorite childhood animated movie. Describe your character and what happens to you in the movie.

The king has called for your head. Just as you're about to be executed, the executioner leans forward and whispers, "don't worry, you're not really going to die."

The ship from the Northern Empire has finally found what it's looking for: The New World - a brand new continent teeming with unique plant and animal life. There are even signs of other humans living there. Everything is great for the explorers, but not for the young stowaway who was expecting a voyage to a much simpler location.

You've spent years climbing the ranks to be able to serve the king. Your plan was to assassinate him once you got close enough, but it turns out the king isn't even a real person.

The adventuring heroes were met with their strangest obstacle yet: a goblin missing an eye, wearing a jester's outfit, and wielding a funny looking sword. "I am Schnoglin," he proclaimed, "and to pass, you must defeat me in my game."

The famous DJ Viole is never seen without her mask. During a live show, a fan runs onto the stage and pulls her mask off, revealing to the world exactly why she has never been seen without it.

**When you blew out your birthday candles this year, you wished you could switch lives with your favorite celebrity. The next morning, you wake up in a different bed.**

You're a famous architect that has been commissioned to design the strangest building ever. It requires secret rooms for odd purposes. It pays well, so you accept the assignment.

You're in college and you've been assigned roommates. One is a superhero, one is a dragon, and one is a time traveler. There's gold all over the apartment, reporters always knocking on the door, and weird people from different eras visiting all the time.

You adopt a cute little puppy from the pound. After a few days, you realize it's a young shapeshifter who continuously changes it's form. You never know what you'll find when you get home each day.

You find a really nice pair of sneakers at the thrift store. When you try them on, you realize they are magical.

Last year you realized that whatever you put into your pot came out tasting delicious. Now you're a very famous celebrity chef. You feel like a fraud.

The money tree in your backyard grows cash every night, as long as you give it what it wants.

The witch that lives in the forest informs you that 50% of the students want the school to disappear. You're the last person to vote, your vote decides whether or not the school will vanish.

You have a magic mirror. When somebody looks into it, you can see what kind of person they are. You decide to use it on some of your best friends and family members.

You have the unique psychic ability to touch someone on the shoulder and see what they will be in the future. You try it on your best friend and are terrified at what you see.

A rat steals the king's crown. What does he do with it?

Every time you close your eyes you see a smiling cat staring at you. You don't know what it means, but you're sure it means something.

You're finally in San Francisco following the directions on the map your best friend drew for you. Suddenly you're in Chinatown. It's noisy, with lots of people in the streets going about their business. You turn down an alleyway and enter a small shop. An old man tells you he's been expecting you, pulls back a silk curtain, and tells you to go inside.

You love playing pranks on people and making people laugh, so the gods bestowed upon you the power to freeze time so you can tie people's shoe laces together and other silly things.

**Choose one of your favorite stories, either your own or someone else's, and write a sequel to it.**

# Your Own Prompts
Write your own ideas for story prompts on the following two pages

# Ideas Page
Use this space to write your ideas for characters, settings, names or anything else you don't want to forget

# Your Notes

Use the following pages for additional notes, or to write a story if you go somewhere and forget to bring a notebook.

# Vocabulary for Fantasy Writers

Use the following words for inspiration. There's a blank page you can use to list your own favorite words for this genre. Better yet, keep a separate notebook that you can dedicate to vocabulary words for this genre or any other genre that you enjoy writing.

| | | |
|---|---|---|
| shiver | frigid | wizard |
| agoraphobia | pandora's box | witch |
| acrophobia | timidly | sorcerer |
| arachnophobia | forcefully | mage |
| mute | shan-gri-la | magic |
| destiny | bedouin | wand |
| enlightened | into the abyss | cloak |
| fantasm | wart | bandit |
| adventure | peg leg | time-travel |
| embark | eye patch | pirate ship |
| voyage | duel | ethereal |
| latitude/longitude | poison | mana |
| north star | first snowfall | hypnotize |
| cartographer | charming | enchant |
| coin toss | desire | divination |
| faster than light | extravaganza | spell |
| daydreams | light vs dark | potion |
| magic academy | tempestuous | demigod |
| summoning | ninja | goblin |
| utopia | samurai | elves |
| barbarian | cult leader | fae |
| vikings | wild west | dragonfly |
| figment | treehouse | mystical |
| grotesque | 10 gallon hat | black cat |
| druid | train robbery | knight in shining armor |
| gothic | toadstool | zombie |
| freelancer | north pole | archer |
| expensive | in disguise | dream walker |
| starving | con artist | crusader |
| power at a price | charlatan | wish |
| hollow | secret society | starry night |
| hallow | aliens | full moon |
| willow tree | martians | eclipse |
| oak tree | upside down | castle |
| palm tree | golden scarab | cruel |
| cheating | in the dark | curse |
| sacrifice | hidden | talking animals |
| responsibility | witching hour | magic carpet |
| immaturity | depraved | labor |
| penance | sour | courtesy |

| | | |
|---|---|---|
| condor | flying machine | chimera |
| messenger | steampunk | fireball |
| reborn | vengeance | cauldron |
| chivalrous | romance | swamp |
| mysterious egg | betrayal | ancient ruins |
| gold | freedom | crypt |
| silver | despair | dungeon |
| ambush | gem stones | desolate |
| torchlight | ambrosia | cellar |
| passageway | plunder | tavern |
| cobblestones | seven seas | quest |
| test of courage | mermaid | prophetic vision |
| waterfall | fountain of youth | owl |
| artifact | nectar | twilight |
| relic | library | mouse |
| legendary | abandoned archives | village |
| stream | vault | drawbridge |
| fatal blow | portal to another world | empire |
| jeopardy | teleportation | abode |
| mountain | meteor | foreboding |
| volcano | extinction | trance |
| secret code | pre-historic | alchemist |
| masquerade ball | pike | philosopher's stone |
| fete | glaive | wyvern |
| bard | mace | werewolf |
| lute | sword | tower |
| lyre | shield | necromancy |
| flute | gambeson | seance |
| painter | dagger | oracle |
| renaissance | inside a whale | troll |
| glitch | Atlantis | cave |
| wormhole | catalyst | highlands |
| poet | scythe | fjords |
| astronomer | paige | chosen one |
| crossbow | red rose | dragon |
| joust | lantern | genie in a bottle |
| lance | healer | divine |
| hot air balloon | the Alps | essence |
| unknown caller | Himalayan Mountains | holy/unholy |
| wedding ring | Sasquatch | mythical |
| looking glass | candlelight | shape shifter |
| leather pouch | black magic | trickster |
| gold coins | outhouse | snake charmer |
| ransom | plague | mirage |
| guard dog | seductive | oasis |
| servants | passport | temple |
| gargoyle | visa | heroic |
| orient | blimp | muse |
| petrified | windmill | vista |
| shocked | eerie | primordial |
| shivering | pale and sickly | beastly |
| peasant | jester | wench |
| nobleman | blacksmith | misty |
| heir to the throne | dwarf | thunderous |
| prince/princess | cloudy | medieval |

| | | |
|---|---|---|
| vagrant | circus | Singapore |
| rainbow | string theory | Manila |
| faustian | energy | Pegasus |
| in the beginning | appear | freckles |
| chaos | disappear | dimples |
| glacier | nuclear | fallen leaves |
| flirtatious | war | snowflakes |
| tribe | tempest | icicles |
| ritual dance | puppet show | blizzard |
| silver tongue | silence | footprints |
| weasel words | skeleton key | chain mail |
| pure | quill and ink | sailor |
| crocodile tears | knickers | scuffle |
| macabre | brass ring | walk the plank |
| medina | nook | cobra |
| kasbah | theory | spider queen |
| monastery | investigator | praying mantis |
| meditate | fancy dress | faraway places |
| victorian | jungle cruise | unorthodox methods |
| bowler hat | The Nile | sneaky |
| startled | jumble sale | underhanded |
| asylum | pharaoh | narcissist |
| plan z | bakery | floating |
| sentimental | tavern | horde |
| last rites | coach | hoard |
| stalk | rice fields | scribe |
| hack and slash | plateau | cleric |
| change the world | orchard | monk |
| last will and testament | nectar | throne |
| graphic | backpack | cochineal bug |
| minimal | bungalow | rose madder |
| violently | penthouse | silk road |
| gently | motel | renaissance |
| maternal instincts | hotel | wicked |
| blood, sweat and tears | inn | wretched |
| only choose one | honeymoon | honorable |
| evil vs evil | French Quarter | virtuous |
| deja vu | Latin Quarter | warm-blooded |
| paranoia | China Town | emotional intelligence |
| hypothetical | Little Italy | bed bugs |
| exotic | Venice | monster under the bed |
| don't go outside | Swiss Alps | mineshaft |
| magi | French Riviera | excavate |
| sultan | Costa del Sol | double-edged sword |
| principal's office | Casablanca | betrothed |
| courtyard | Marrakech | Kraken |
| moat | Hagia Sophia | arranged marriage |
| jagged edge | Santorini | nuptials |
| serrated | Berlin | oath |
| equestrian | St. Petersburg | allegiance to the crown |
| champion | Tokyo | fable |
| keepsake | Johannesburg | tragedy |
| heirloom | Alexandria | newspaper article |
| foggy night | Luxor | Timbuktu |
| moon shadows | Zimbabwe | Zanzibar |

# Your Vocabulary List

# Common Grammatical Mistakes

it's - it is - "it's a great day for a picnic" is the same as "it is a great day for a picnic"
its - without an apostrophe is possessive (something belonging to it)

there's - there is - "There's so much food!"
they're - they are - "They're coming with us."
their - possessive - "That's their ball."

a lot - is always two words, never "alot"

your - possessive - "That's your sandwich."
you're - you are - "You're my best friend."

effect - end result - "Let's hope the speech has a positive effect on them."
affect - means to effect - "I was affected by what happened to me."

advice - is something you give to someone - "My mother always has great advice."
advise - is something you do to someone - "I advise you to stop doing that."

possessive singular - "That's my horse's food."
possessive plural - "All the horses' food is gone!"

correct way to use "I" and "me" - use I before a verb
"Aiden and I ate lunch late today." Hint: take away the other person to see how it sounds. For example: "I ate lunch today." sounds right. You wouldn't say "Me ate lunch today."

Use "me" when you're receiving something. For example: "Give the letter to me please." So, you would say "give the letter to John and me when you're done with it please." Double check by saying it without the other person. You wouldn't say "give the letter back to I" so you should always use "me" here. Using myself is also wrong.

Use "too" only in place of also or when stating excess. "I like them too!" and "This cake is too sweet."

Made in the USA
Columbia, SC
02 May 2023